PANIC'S HYMN

PANIC'S HYMN

DUANE ESPOSITO

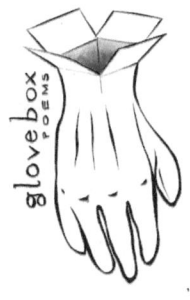

Panic's Hymn
©2018 by Duane Esposito
All rights reserved

GloveBox Poems
First Edition

A version of this was originally published under the title *Cadillac Battleship* by brokenTribe Press (2005).

ISBN 978-1-943899-07-4

GloveBox Poems
San Diego, CA

ACKNOWLEDGMENTS

My heartfelt thanks go to Adam Deutsch, managing editor of GloveBox Poems, for his work to bring this reissue / reimagining to publication. Thank you for your dedication to poetry, for devoting the time it deserves to exist in the world.

To the deep readers, the crazed seekers whose insights were crucial for the completion of this book: Anthony Piccione, Lisa Esposito, mom, Ralph Nazareth, William Heyen, Jon Palzer, Li-Young Lee, Jay Auerfeld, Adam Deutsch, Manny Nomikos, Adam Haridopolos, & Sheida Dayani: thank you one & all. "We are the music makers, & we are the dreamers of dreams." As well, I'm indebted to Dennis Cooper for his clarity & sincerity, & to maxxiantu for his spirited, unwaivering support of this work, for being trustworthy & dedicated to professionalism & precision.

I would also like to thank the editors of the following magazines & anthologies, in which some of these poems (or earlier versions of them, often with different titles) appeared. Current titles are listed here. As well, many times poems drastically change during rewrites, get resubmitted in their new form, &— subsequently— some poems listed here have been accepted twice.

Access Literature: "Open Window" & "Love"; *BlazeVOX:* "The Closest It's Been To Earth in Fifty Thousand Years," "Sing," & "Sky"; *Can We Have Our Ball Back:* "Love Poem" , "Geese," & "Beauty"; *Clare:* "Praise" ; *Faultline:* "Safe"; *Fence:* "Particulars" & "Beauty"; *Into the Teeth of the Wind:* "Blessing"; *Snow Monkey:* "Open" & "Prayer"; *Spinning Jenny:* "Home"; *Wisconsin Review:* "Marriage" & "I Want to Feel You"

For Lisa, my love: joy.
& for Tony (1939-2001), who lit the interior: faith.

CONTENTS

I

1 Stroke
2 Geese
4 Helpless
5 Therapy-Blue
7 Weakness
8 Impact
10 Blessing

II

15 Love Poem
16 Home
17 Open Window
18 Marriage
19 I Want to Feel You
20 The Dark-Faced Girl in the Front Row of my Intro to Literature Class
21 Things You Should Know
22 The Chair
23 Too Much
24 Southwestern Simile

III

29 Ride
30 Beloved
32 Particulars
33 Love
35 Open
37 Prayer
38 Why Not Capitalize Frog?
40 The Closest It's Been to Earth
   in Fifty-Thousand Years
42 Sky
43 Gone
44 Safe
45 Beauty
46 Sing
47 Praise

49 About the Author

"He carried his crippled arm now
the way a king might carry a scepter."
-Harry Crews

I

Stroke

An unseen thread from
brain to limbs divides me,

the right side fine, but the left,
even its bones, shakes

into my malformed boyhood,
& the left-body convulses

with the brain's right side.
This gets close to infantile.

Stroke: a mark upon my institution.
Poor architectural construction.

Geese

I'm half passed out from booze,
& one guy forces me to suck his cock.

My hemiplegic body
can't be my protector,

right arm tied
behind my back,

stiff-limbed, heroic in winter, & I
don't tend toward loving my body.

A glass half-filled with mildewed soda
my friends force me to drink.

Clouds touch land in silence.
Geese in dream sleep near my head,

webbed feet twitch as
they rest against my neck.

I wake to sunrise on the Hudson &
a glass-window-view of me bent & paralyzed.

Memory's hysterical history:
where's half my body?

Five soft fingers.
Five rubbery bones.

Spastic wrist position.
One shaky leg.

Toes don't move.
One side leans.

Tight ankle joint.
Immobile shoulder pulls.

Genius is my motion
through space.

Helpless

A kid named Kovacs
from up the street slams
my face into the grass,

demands I drink a glass
filled with sour milk,
shoves moist cat food

into my mouth,
ties me to a rope,
& drags me bleeding.

To scar myself with shame, I cut
my testicles with a toenail clipper,
a reptile waits for shadows to fade.

But my friend Fay
hears what Kovacs did
& jacks his ass against

the handball wall
in the field behind
Candlewood High,

another place I've been abused
far too often by
too many kids half my size.

Therapy-Blue

I mean to beat you with my bony arm,
crack the dexterous hands you used
to twist my limbs into mobility.

I mean to slash your skin,
cut your tongue
in spirals underneath,

decorate the ground
with this thin flesh, & suck
the oxygen from your muscles.

I mean to eviscerate your bowels, & drag
your bloodied corpse
across the therapy-blue mats

stained by drool
from palsy-mouthed girls
& crippled boys.

Life rearranged.
Immobile mind
deprived, & I

mean to conspire
with your eyes to see
me at eight in treatment lying

face down on a beach ball,
right arm tied behind my back,
you grab my ankles,

push me forward, no good arm
to stop my face from slamming
the stiff & sweaty floor.

I must bite your sinews
until the roots itch & hum
& you imbibe my boyhood

pressure to become
your whole body,
to accept— while I despise—

your filthy tactics. Dear physical therapist,
I mean to force you to sing— inside
your brain— the fugue of my half-self.

Weakness

I limp home in winter—
spastic leg hikes behind,

right hand holds a bottle,
I fall & crack my elbow.

Other arm can't reach
to ease the frozen ground.

Head hits too. Blood
pours out the ear canal.

Will I learn to walk normally again?
Will reflex reenter my arm?

In a dream that night, five
ants in the shape of a star

sit motionless on my skin,
& I punch my cat's face: it tilts

from side to side as fluid spits
out its ears, right before it dies.

Impact

20 years after being abandoned
by his mother, my father fights

at Iwo Jima. He comes
home shell-shocked.

After he marries
& they have kids,

he hangs on corners
& lusts young girls

with my mother at home on
the phone with his shrink.

His children need
powder & a thick

towel after a bath
in the steel sink.

I'm six— kicking one
balloon into the ceiling.

Only on the good days
does he build me a kite or model car.

Only on the good days does he
stare amazed by pigeons flying

at the little league ball game
in the sky between cloud & ground.

Blessing

As mothers in robes with wings
swoop from clouds
of human ash,
fangs puncture psyches,

my dark-faced lover,
nose curved down,
builds walls around
our four-post bed.

We sit inside on pillows, safe.
She rubs her nipples, &
I mutilate her body,
one limb at a time.

Morning rises in my head:
sharp, metallic brain-points,
the horror of waking,
zero power, so I

tear skin from
the red tongue of
the newly tattooed
dog on my left forearm.

Pain tilts: a loon on
a white-capped lake.
I'm sorry for the stardust
that led to creation.

II

Love Poem

My love's nails are bitten
down to skin, her cuticles
torn & bleeding.

Her haircuts are metaphors
for a mutilated psyche,
our mostly dismal bed,

& I can't take my cock
out of my hands—
the itching stinking—
transcend pornography,
these women of one dimension.

What's our relationship?
What are our compulsions?
Dope, poems, sports, booze,
a glass of milk on the windowsill.

She's ninety-three pounds.
She panics over food,
sees tragedy in flowers.

Home

Because you go for walks,
think you're losing weight
off an hysterical stomach,
my fear's armed with anger.

Because you dropped four pounds,
down to ninety-two or so,
I'm afraid of touching
your shoulder blades & hips.

& we don't celebrate
the way we used to,
& I want to move,
with heavy ecstasy,

over any chick with
dreadlocks, a magical ass,
& breasts I can suck
for a good eternity.

& I want to finger &
rub the curving waist
of any young woman
at any university bar.

But I'm going home.
There's a jazz guitarist
on a subway platform
at one thirty-seven
on a Sunday, summer night.

Open Window

You believe you are obese
at 96 pounds, refuse

to consume pleasure,
& because you're cold

our door isn't open,
our joy's untenable.

Love's memory scatters—
flat in me while you speak,

& I'm carefully distracted by
the sound of the sudden rain.

Marriage

Every weekend we fuck
around with the closet.

(written with Lisa)

I Want to Feel You

But I
only have
one arm

& it's
trapped beneath
your head.

The Dark-Faced Girl in the Front Row of my Intro to Literature Class

She doesn't shave her legs,
& that makes me nervous.

Things You Should Know

Some people come home
& take their shirts off.

I come home &
take my pants off.

The Chair

The substantial dental hygienist,
barely twenty-five, leans over

& digs her tool
into my bleeding gums.

I know this pain,
her touching me,

& maybe we
could close the door,

recline the chair,
& fuck a while.

She goes on cleaning,
but we're really bathing,

sucking wine off each other,
listening to our shadows.

"Rinse, please," she says as
she backs away from the chair.

That sweet perfume must be
in the crease beneath her breasts.

"All finished Duane—
teeth & gums look fine."

Does she smell herself? Does she
know what odor does to me?

Too Much

A blond woman in
a tight red shirt &

pants low on
her late teen hips,

midriff exposed,
belly button ring,

one tattoo on
well-tanned skin,

walks into my room,
confused, looking for hers.

My class watches how
I contain my reaction,

& I'm thinking of the wonders
I know she knows she has.

God's all over me. I can't get it off,
& I'd like to teach her about the cosmos,

if I was twenty-five,
with a bottle of wine,

"Some Girls" by the Stones,
a black light, no paranoia, & time.

Southwestern Simile

I love my wife like Texas
loves the death penalty.

III

"Knowing when to git off a dog
is as smart as when to git on."
                    -Harry Crews

Ride

One 15-inch / 50 caliber gun's
mounted on the hood.
The hair trigger's cocked—

chamber smoke tinted.
I'm blank & failing
as the dashboard vibrates

freedom & terror.
I shove my fist
into the memory

of another's face—
ignore humanity.
I hum panic's hymn.

Beloved

While I caress your thigh,
my left two limbs, half-wit brains,

dictate I can't ever be sturdy,
& control covers humiliation,

grief in body,
shame in body

hit & rearranged, & I
crave to pin you down,

bra left on for blowjob.
Work that ass with thumb.

I grab your face,
force your mouth,

& you who loved to please
now fear pleasure.

I'm asleep inside the gazer
& the body being seen.

East River currents
& barges go by,

& you, my beloved,
these days together—

thunder storms approach,
how long since the sun?—

I fail your body—
grief-shouts in a concrete hallway.

Particulars

Evolution surely
gives up on us all,

our loves & triumphs,
our planet-wide distress,

our knowledge of our losses
strangled in our heads, &—

in usual ways—
I admire beauty:

wind, rain down
the dark hallway.

Quiet inside.
Smile arrives.

Nose silhouetted
behind closed eyes.

Rising circles of light,
this brain: my heart's

illuminate mind.

Love

Will you dance to Run
DMC & Public Enemy?

Will you draw, again,
that skinny chicken,

whose beak's tied on with string,
& the fat Turkey Hero

in sneakers & cape, who flies
to rescue the withering bird?

Are you falling or ascending?
Are you tiresome & cold?

Is God our awareness
inward of it

or its projection
outward into us,

blessed or mawkish hearts
silhouetted inside our chests?

Love, will you watch with me—
even while traffic & trains

whirl in the background—
geese at the end of winter

on the ball field out field,
& in the sumps?

Will you lean toward the sound
of the shaping of our grief?

Open

For joy, for fucking,
for female forms,

& not for your
time-bound ego,

smell her after a shower,
watch her hair slowly dry.

Smile when she mentions
the North Shore beaches,

sandwiches, wine,
& summer unwound.

Walk with her.
Smoke sweet dope.

Talk about massage &
the flesh above the eye.

Stare at her body,
hapless & waking object,

the joyous prospect
of no one finding fault.

Lean into a moist ease
with hope & no door to no hell-

room ever opening.
A frog hops by.

Trust the unfathomable questions
you can't find language to ask,

& don't feel empty—
even as your lover's

consumed by shame. Breathe
the shadow-play of cosmos & history

created before our breath—
the Universe & how to ride.

Prayer

Maybe, God, your hairy legs
hang into my far-back-brain

where ideas are only shadows
& there is no access to Truth.

Maybe you curl your lengthy toes,
just before I sleep.

Maybe you grab hold
of a wider human being.

Why Not Capitalize Frog?

Is faith an attempt to near our odd behaviors,
lovers of questions, plumbed of spirit?
Does another's untapped psyche
remind us of ourselves— ugly & in the way?
Is it all as plain as 14 billion years
of Universe creation, 4 billion years
of Planet formation, 4 million years
of Human evolution, & we've simply
failed to wake to miracles?

When pressed in my profession
where soul's passé, I stand wild
for the transcendental.
This is not polemical.
We rocket about a thousand
miles per hour, & still our language
fades at the speed of horror,
this life defined by time—
a stiff-legged & headless crow
on its back on any street.

How— through media, breasts,
& pectorals, the young adjusting genitals
& fingering their phones, blank
& arrogant, the dread, bathetic soul—
do we believe in Godliness?
How to eat? How to smell?

Must we dig at seeming perfection,
desire & dissection, withdraw
into silence, construct our borders,
like bodies ground into a cloud-filled sky?

Are fantasies distractions from
or extensions of the unconscious?

Can't we believe in Whitman?
Can't we believe in Blake?
Can't we believe in Emerson,
Dickinson, Nietzsche, & me?
Capitalize God. Frog
hops in back yard:
Frog as God. Why
not capitalize Frog?

The Closest It's Been to Earth in Fifty-Thousand Years

1

My brain vessel explodes, & three
days later, after waking from a coma,
I'm in a wheelchair on the rooftop

of a hospital, left shoulder propped
by brace beneath armpit, left leg falls
from the metal foot plate,

head tilts, spastic, to one side,
spittle dried in the corner
of my slurring mouth.

2

The years since your eleventh,
comparing elbows, upper arms,
cutting crusts off bread.

An interior voice that says
you're obese for eating &
don't deserve your pleasures.

The afternoons dizzy, the nights
asleep early, eating only vegetables
to deny your taste for meat.

3

Are clouds the color of a heart
in a bay at low tide?
May we wash the sky into our faces?

To be both
the living &
the life being seen,

before time & after, creation
from damage— in memory
of our trauma.

Aren't we alive?
Mars floats by
our bedroom window.

Sky

Running after kids
who vandalize our home.

Driving his milk truck
to pay off the mortgage.

Punching holes in walls
& hanging pictures.

Distracted from family
by t.v.— dinner

at half-time each
fall for 16 weeks.

He kicks failed dreams
through a private snow.

May the Universe bless
& keep my father.

Gone

29 years after the final
act of my father's love,

I no longer believe
my crippled arm—

now tattooed "like a dog"—
caused him to leave.

A breath I'm calm for taking,
a downward turn into a world,

a gasp in the before-time,
a song of space in the after.

The sea's fierce echo
in my skull & limbs.

Ancient trauma,
psyche & body, moves

a little, & he vanishes
in the twilight horizon.

Safe

Her hip bones protrude.
Her legs are teenage in size.
I enter her on top of me,
use my one good hand,

these gorilla fingers,
to feel her breasts— a girl's
ribbed chest. Do I like
the nipples blue with veins?

My thin leg shakes—
a wire tightening.
The love between
the cripple & the anorexic.

We sleep spooned
into each other,
beyond our harmed bodies,
& she dreams she's crashing

planes into oceans.
I grab her neck & hold
her loving head
above the salty water.

Beauty

When the night comes
love's a place of horror,
guard dogs on the roof,
black bugs on the floor nearby,
bodies hung outside the window.

We hold each other, terrified.
It's a good life, Universe,
hands dipped in sea,
the love-smile arrives.
I hope your eggs move.

Sing

We are big or just enough space.
Are these two things the same?

Is this our time,
brushing your hair?

Is this a kind of prayer,
useless limbs with wings

to lift them
far from fury?

My dreams are filled
with top hats on polished floors.

Has the bulb been planted with these fingers?
Is each year an answer that it has?

Praise

Horrified by raccoons
with partially crushed heads,
on the roadside gulping

& squirrels dead
from broken necks,
twisted spinal places,

we lie down into
our bodies,
lives thrown off

the trauma-road.
At the line where eyelids
meet when closed,

a river widens,
& we float to mountains
on my forehead.

Kisses. Circles. Rainstorms.
Heads fold together.
We are no ugly heart.

There is praise.
We are safe.
We sleep like this.

ABOUT THE AUTHOR

Duane Esposito is a Professor of English at Nassau Community College in Garden City, New York. He has an M.A. from SUNY Brockport and an M.F.A. from the University of Arizona. His work was selected by Diane Glancy for an Academy of American Poets Award & over the years his poems have been published in dozens of journals. His collections are *The Book of Bubba* (Brown Dog Press, 1998), *Cadillac Battleship* (brokenTribe Press, 2005), *Declaration for Your Bones* (Yuganta Press, 2012), & *Dropping Death*, a collaboration with Ralph Nazareth (Yuganta Press, 2018). *Panic's Hymn* (GloveBox Poems, 2018) is a reissue / reimagining of *Cadillac Battleship*. He lives on Long Island—on Lopsided Farm— with his wife, daughter, son, & many animals.

www.ingramcontent.com/pod-product-compliance
Lightning Source LLC
Chambersburg PA
CBHW021452080526
44588CB00009B/812